Every Kid's Guide to
Coping With
Childhood Traumas

Written by

JOY BERRY

GROLIER ENTERPRISES INC.
Danbury, Connecticut

About the Author and Publisher

Joy Berry's mission in life is to help families cope with everyday problems and to help children become competent, responsible, happy individuals. To achieve her goal, she has written over two hundred self-help books for children from infancy through age twelve. Her work has revolutionized children's publishing by providing families with practical, how-to, living skills information that was previously unavailable in children's books.

Joy has gathered a dedicated team of experts, including psychologists, educators, child developmentalists, writers, editors, designers, and artists to form her publishing company and to help produce her work.

The company, Living Skills Press, produces thoroughly researched books and audiovisual materials that successfully combine humor and education to teach children subjects ranging from how to clean a bedroom to how to resolve problems and get along with other people.

Managing Editor: Ellen Klarberg
Copy Editors: Kate Dickey, Annette Gooch, Susan Starbird
Contributing Editors: Libby Byers, Maureen Dryden, Yona Flemming,
James Gough, M.D., Gretchen Savidge
Editorial Assistant: Lana Eberhard

Art Director: Laurie Westdahl
Designer: Laurie Westdahl
Illustration Designer: Bartholomew
Inking Artist: Rashida Tessler
Coloring Artist: Rashida Tessler
Lettering Artist: Rashida Tessler
Production Artist: Gail Miller

Typographer: Communication Graphics

Because you are a person, you will most likely experience trauma sometime during your lifetime.

Every Kid's Guide to Coping With Childhood Traumas will help you understand the following:

- trauma and traumatic experiences,
- losing something valuable,
- going to a new school,
- failing at doing something important,
- being separated from family members,
- staying in the hospital,
- moving,
- divorce,
- the death of someone,
- serious illness or injury, and
- the six steps for handling childhood trauma.

Physical or emotional pain that hurts a lot is called **trauma.** Anything that causes trauma is called a **_traumatic experience._**

If you are like most children, you will encounter certain traumatic experiences either directly or indirectly.

Traumatic experiences that you encounter *directly* involve you personally.

Traumatic experiences that you encounter *indirectly* do not involve you, but they involve someone you know.

Whether you encounter a traumatic experience directly or indirectly, it will have either a positive or negative effect on your life.

If you respond to a traumatic situation in a positive way, it will most likely have a positive effect on your life.

If you respond to a traumatic situation in a negative way, it will most likely have a negative effect on your life.

The information in this book can help you respond to traumatic experiences in positive ways. It can also help you be patient, understanding, and kind to others who have encountered a traumatic experience.

Sometimes people lose something that is valuable to them.

Losing something that is valuable to you can be a traumatic experience.

People who lose something that is valuable to them often feel
- **frustrated** because they cannot find the object,
- **angry** at themselves or someone else for losing it,
- **disappointed** that they will not be able to use the object again,
- **sad** that it is gone, and
- **worried** that they will not be able to replace the lost object.

If you should lose something that is valuable to you, you can make yourself feel better by doing your best to find it.

- Return to where you last saw the object and search for it.
- Make a thorough search of the places where you used the object.
- Ask people to help you find the object.

If you are unable to find the object, you can make yourself feel better by doing whatever you can to get over the loss.

■ Give yourself a specific amount of time to find the object and stop looking for it when the allotted time has passed.

■ Figure out if and how the object can be replaced, and then replace it as soon as possible.

■ Try not to focus on the missing object. Instead, think of the things you still have and be thankful for them.

Sometimes it is necessary for children to go to a school they have not attended before.

Going to a new school can be a traumatic experience.

Children who must go to a new school often feel

■ *insecure* because they do not know what they will be doing or what will happen to them at the new school,

■ *worried* that they will not be able to do what is expected of them,

■ *worried* that they will not be accepted or liked by the people at the new school, and

■ *worried* that they will not like going to the new school.

When you must go to a new school, you can make yourself feel better by doing these things:

With the help of your parents, learn all you can about the new school. Find out about the

- school calendar (opening and closing dates, vacations and holidays),
- daily schedule (when things happen every day),
- rules (what you can and cannot do),
- dress codes (what you can and cannot wear),
- food program (what food, if any, is available),
- facilities (where everything is located),
- curriculum (what you will study), and
- personnel (who works at the school).

You can get this information by visiting the new school, telephoning or writing to the school office, or talking to students who attend the school.

Do whatever you can do to make attending the new school a positive experience. If possible, get to know the people, the school, and its surroundings before you start attending the new school.

- Call the school office and make an appointment to visit the school.
- Ask to see your future classroom and meet your future teacher.
- Take a list of your questions with you when you visit.
- Make sure all your questions are answered before your visit is finished.
- Ask for printed information about the school that you can take home and read.
- Gather together all the supplies you will need at least one week before you begin school.

Do these things after you begin school:

- Make at least one friend at school as soon as possible.
- Attend the school for at least one month before making up your mind about it.

Sometimes people fail when they try to do something that is important to them.

Failing at doing something that is important to you can be a traumatic experience.

People who fail at doing something that is important to them often feel

- **defeated** because they think that failing makes them losers,
- **disappointed** that they could not accomplish what they tried to accomplish,
- **inferior** because they do not think they are as good as people who succeed,
- **frustrated** that they were unable to do something they needed or wanted to do,
- **embarrassed** because they think that failure makes them appear to be stupid or incompetent,
- **guilty** because they think they did not try hard enough, and
- **worried** that they will never succeed.

If you fail at doing something important, you can make
yourself feel better by doing these things:

- Remember the things you can do well.
- Remember that no one is perfect. Every person
  fails at one time or another.
- Realize that failure can give you an opportunity to
  learn from your mistake. If you failed because you
  did something wrong, you can learn to avoid doing
  the same thing again. If you failed because you
  neglected to do something, you can learn to do it
  the next time.

- Avoid focusing on your failures. Instead, focus on the lessons to be learned from the experience.
- Avoid being impatient with yourself. Thinking of yourself as a failure will only make you feel as though you cannot do anything right. You will not be able to do your best when you feel this way. You might not be able to succeed if you do not do your best.
- Avoid giving up or thinking that you are a failure.

Sometimes people temporarily leave members of their families, or members of their families temporarily leave them.

Being separated from family members can be a traumatic experience.

Children who are separated from their families often feel

- *angry* that they are separated from the people in their families,
- *afraid* that they might get hurt because their parents are not around to protect them,
- *insecure* because they do not know what is going to happen to them while they are away from their families,
- *worried* that something might prevent them from reuniting with their families,
- *left out* because they are unable to participate in whatever their families are doing, and
- *lonely* because they miss being around their families.

If you are ever separated from members of your family, you can make yourself feel better by doing these things:

Find out
- how long the separation will last (when it will begin and end),
- where you will be and what you will be doing during the separation,
- where the members of your family will be and what they will be doing during the separation,
- how you will be able to contact the members of your family, and
- when and how your family members will contact you.

You can get this information by talking to your parents or the adults who are responsible for you during the separation.

Do whatever you can do to make the separation a
positive experience.

- Give the members of your family a pleasant
  good-bye.
- Keep yourself busy with positive activities during
  the separation.
- Talk to other people about your family whenever
  you miss them.
- If possible, telephone or write letters to the people
  in your family.
- Use a calendar to help you keep track of the
  separation (mark off each day).
- Think about the happy day when you will be getting
  back together with your family.

Sometimes people with serious illnesses or injuries must stay in the hospital.

Staying in the hospital can be a traumatic experience.

People who must stay in the hospital often feel
- *fearful* because they don't know exactly what is going to happen to them,
- *worried* that whatever happens to them will be painful,
- *isolated* because they are away from their family and friends,
- *homesick* because they are away from home and familiar surroundings,
- *bored* because their activities are often limited, and
- *frustrated* because they cannot do the things they normally do every day.

If you should have to stay in the hospital, you can make yourself feel better by learning all you can about the hospital. Find out

- what will happen to you while you are in the hospital,
- what you can and cannot do while you are there, and
- how long you will be staying there.

You can get this information by talking to people such as your parents, your doctors and nurses, and other hospital workers. You can also get some of this information by reading about hospitals.

Do whatever you need to do to make your stay in the hospital beneficial and pleasant for yourself.

■ If possible, get to know the people and the surroundings by visiting the hospital before you stay there.

■ Bring things from home (such as favorite toys, books, and projects).

■ Ask your family and friends to visit you as often as they can.

■ Discuss your thoughts and feelings honestly with your parents, your doctors, and the hospital workers.

■ Cooperate fully with your parents and the hospital workers.

Sometimes people have to move from one home to another.

Moving can be a traumatic experience.

People who have to move often feel

■ *insecure* because they do not know what is going
   to happen to them in the new location,

■ *worried* that they won't like living in the new
   location,

■ *sad* that they will be leaving the people and places
   that are familiar to them, and

■ *overwhelmed and frustrated* because they have
   to start over, make new friends, and develop a
   whole new life.

If you should have to move, you can make yourself feel better by learning all you can about your new home and neighborhood *before* you move. Find out about the

■ school you will attend,

■ church or synagogue you might attend, and

■ community programs and activities available to people your age.

You can learn about your new community by visiting it or by contacting its chamber of commerce.

Do whatever you can to make the move go as
smoothly as possible.

Do these things before you move:

■ Get the addresses and telephone numbers of your
  special friends and neighbors so you can keep in
  touch with them.
■ Collect photographs and mementos from the
  community you will be leaving. Store these items in
  a scrapbook or special box.
■ Help your family pack. Be sure to pack your own
  belongings.

Do these things after you move:

■ Unpack your own belongings and set up your own
  bedroom.
■ Make new friends and get involved in your
  community as soon as possible.
■ Concentrate on what you like about the new
  community.
■ Telephone or write letters to your special friends
  and neighbors from the old community.
■ Look at photographs and mementos from the old
  community.

Sometimes a husband and wife decide they do not want to be married any longer, and they get a divorce.

A divorce can be a traumatic experience.

The children of parents who get a divorce often feel

- *insecure* because they do not know what is going to happen to them,
- *rejected* by the parent who will not be living with them,
- *guilty* because they feel they might have done something to cause the divorce,
- *confused* because they do not know which parent to side with,
- *cheated* because they cannot be a part of what they consider to be a "normal" family with a mother and father,
- *angry* at their parents for getting a divorce, and
- *hopeful* that their parents might get back together again.

If your parents get a divorce, you can make yourself feel better by doing these things:

- Realize that your situation is not unique. There are many children whose parents are divorced.
- Realize that there will always be someone to help care for you while you are a child.
- Remember that your parents' divorce is something between them.
- Remember that your parents' divorce has not been caused by you.
- Avoid getting involved in your parents' arguments.
- Do not try to decide who is right or wrong. Do not take sides.

Do whatever you can do to make the best of the situation. Make sure both your parents know

■ which parent you want to live with and
■ when you want to see the parent who does not live with you.

Talk to a caring adult if you are unable to share this information with your parents. Then ask the adult to talk with your parents.

Keep in touch with the parent who does not live with you.

■ Call the parent on the telephone.
■ Write letters to the parent.
■ Help make plans for getting together with the parent.

Accept the fact that your parents' divorce is most likely final and that they will probably not get back together again.

Sometimes people you know die.

The death of someone you know can be a traumatic experience.

When someone has died, the people who knew the person often feel

- **_fearful_** that they might die too,
- **_worried_** that someone close to them might also die,
- **_sad_** that they will never again be able to see the person who died,
- **_guilty_** that they didn't treat the person better when he or she was alive,
- **_angry_** that the person died and left them, and
- **_lonely_** because they cannot be with the person who died.

If someone you know should die, you can make
yourself feel better by doing these things:

■ Learn all you can about the person's death. Find out
what caused the person to die and what you can do
to possibly avoid having the same thing happen to
you. You can get this information by talking to your
parents and the family and friends of the person
who died.

- Do whatever you can to work through your feelings about the person's death.
- Let yourself cry and feel sad for as long as you need to.
- Share your thoughts and feelings honestly with people who care.
- Do something in honor of the person who died (write a letter, a poem, or story; draw some pictures; make a scrapbook). You might want to share your project with other people, or you might prefer to keep the project to yourself.
- Concentrate on the pleasant memories of the person.

Sometimes people become very sick and their illness threatens their lives or well-being. Sometimes people become injured and their injury threatens their lives or well-being.

A serious illness or injury that threatens a person's life or well-being can be a traumatic experience.

People who have a serious illness or injury often feel

- *uncomfortable* because of the pain caused by the illness or injury,
- *fearful* that they might get worse or might not heal,
- *worried* that they might not be the same as they were before the illness or injury,
- *angry* that the illness or injury happened to them, and
- *frustrated* because the illness or injury limits what they can do.

If you should become sick or injured, you can make yourself feel better by learning all you can about your illness or injury. Find out

- what caused the illness or injury,
- what can be done to help your body heal itself, and
- what can be done to keep the illness or injury from happening again.

You can get this information by talking to people such as your parents and doctors. You can also become informed by reading.

Do whatever you need to do to help your body heal itself.

- Get plenty of rest.
- Eat the right kinds of food and drink the right kinds of beverages.
- Take the proper medications.
- Do whatever your parents and your doctors say you should do.
- Picture yourself being well again.

The traumatic experiences that you encounter directly need to be handled appropriately. Following these six steps will help you deal with traumatic experiences.

Step 1. Face it.
Admit that you are experiencing trauma. Admit that you are in pain. Don't pretend that you are OK.

Step 2. Accept it.
Accept the fact that the trauma is not going to go away immediately. Realize that you are going to experience some pain for a while.

Step 3. Think about it.
Try to answer these questions:

- What happened to cause this trauma?
- What is going to happen to me?

Step 4. Decide what to do.

Ask yourself these questions:

- What can I do to make the situation better?
- What can I do to make myself feel better?
- What can I do to help the other people who are involved in this situation feel better?

Make sure that whatever you decide to do is not harmful to yourself or others.

Step 5. Do what you have decided to do.

Step 6. Talk about your thoughts and feelings.
It is important that you continue talking about your thoughts and feelings until you feel better.

Don't think that talking just one time about a traumatic experience will make everything OK. It might take you as long as six months or even a year to get all your questions answered and feel better.

Try to be patient with yourself and other people who have encountered a traumatic experience.

Traumatic experiences are upsetting, but if they are handled properly, they can help you
- learn valuable lessons,
- grow, and
- become a better person.